The
Right *Place*
at the
Right *Time*

The Right Place at the Right Time

Stories from a Life in Education

Curtis Connaughty

iUniverse

THE RIGHT PLACE AT THE RIGHT TIME
STORIES FROM A LIFE IN EDUCATION

iUniverse books may be ordered through booksellers or by contacting:

iUniverse
1663 Liberty Drive
Bloomington, IN 47403
www.iuniverse.com
1-800-Authors (1-800-288-4677)

Because of the dynamic nature of the Internet, any web addresses or links contained in this book may have changed since publication and may no longer be valid. The views expressed in this work are solely those of the author and do not necessarily reflect the views of the publisher, and the publisher hereby disclaims any responsibility for them.

Any people depicted in stock imagery provided by Thinkstock are models, and such images are being used for illustrative purposes only.
Certain stock imagery © Thinkstock.

ISBN: 978-1-5320-1658-5 (sc)
ISBN: 978-1-5320-1656-1 (hc)
ISBN: 978-1-5320-1657-8 (e)

Library of Congress Control Number: 2017902532

Print information available on the last page.

iUniverse rev. date: 04/22/2017

To Mary, my wife, my companion for more than sixty years of marriage. I thank her for so many things, like her helpful support during my education career. She was a gracious spectator in sports during my coaching days and still supports me in my athletic interests. I credit her for my long life due to her cooking of healthy foods and convincing me that too many potato chips are not good. She also is the mother of our five children, grandmother of ten, and great-grandmother to six. I love her dearly.

Contents

Foreword

. . . .

This story is about a young man's journey to become a teacher. It involves leaving the farm and finding jobs to pay tuition at a teacher's college. There were many: skinning mink, stone quarry driver, railroad worker, candy factory employee, and soldier.

Six years after starting college, interrupted by two years in the army, he graduated with a bachelor of science degree. He was then hired to teach. There were many challenges, successes, and disappointments during his coaching, teaching, and administrative careers.

The place he chose was everything. The students were everything. His family was everything.

Acknowledgments

· ·

To Mary, my wife, for her understanding and patience and support. Appreciation to the students I came in contact with over the thirty-plus years I was active within the school. I appreciate youth's energy and the points of view of developing minds and bodies.

Our children for their support and love. Their patience with me and their fellow students were appreciated.

To Harlan Leopold, former teacher and wrestling coach, for his wisdom of technology. Without his expertise, this manuscript would not have gotten to the publisher. Thank you for keeping me on task.

George Schell was helpful and key in completing the manuscript. The time we spent together editing is appreciated. George is a retired English teacher.

To Eden Prairie Historical Society, and Ann Higgins, for providing school yearbooks for the pictures. The yearbooks were very helpful in telling my story.

To the teachers and staff of the Eden Prairie School that I had the privilege to work with over the past sixty years.

To Eden Prairie Schools for allowing me to print the pictures from the yearbooks from 1955 to 1986. Appreciation for allowing me the opportunity of belonging to the faculty all those years.

CHAPTER 1

The Early Years

I grew up on Holstein dairy farms neighboring St. Charles, Minnesota, the gateway to Whitewater State Park, east of Rochester, Minnesota. I emphasize Holstein because, as a little boy, I always remember the neighboring farmers arguing which breed gave most milk: Jersey, Guernsey, Brown Swiss, or Holstein. I lived with my mother, father, and sister, Beverly, until 1949. When I was a senior in high school, my brother was born.

My mother suffered complications during my delivery in 1931. The doctor told her not to have any more children. This brought many concerns during her new pregnancy. I knew Mother and Dad went to the hospital that morning. Later on in the day, my father interrupted my high school class and told me I had a brother, whom they had named Gary. He let me know that everything was okay and both were healthy. The news was such a relief. I was so excited I bought a box of cigars, went back to school, and gave every teacher a cigar.

I didn't see my brother Gary as much as I would have liked because I went away to college when he was an infant and then into the army for two years. I went back to college after the army and then settled in Eden Prairie, 120 miles away. Since then, we have made up for lost time.

During the Depression, my family's first farm was located four miles south of Utica, Minnesota. The farm was owned by a dentist, Dr. Wooley, who lived in the upper level of our farmhouse. His practice was in a porch-like addition. He would come to meals from his upstairs room down a firefighter's pole. Seems strange, but he was great to Beverly and me. He built a pond and a small boat so we could paddle around in the pond. He would bring candy when he went to town, but it was always horehound candy, which tasted terrible. My sister and I played tricks on him a few times because of his choice of candy.

My sister Beverly was two years older and liked teasing and giving me just enough ideas to get me in trouble with my mom. She was always coming up with things that I should do even though she knew what my mother would think. I returned the favor a few times when we were in high school.

Grandpa Calhoun, Beverly and Curt

When I first learned to drive, I was not at the required driving age. As a farmer's son, age thirteen, I was permitted to drive a truck loaded with grain or corn to the grain elevator in St. Charles. Because I was driving at such an early age, all the young girls wanted to ride with me: their first ride without parents.

Once, I dropped Beverly off at a phone booth while I drove another girl home. The trip took longer than expected, so when I returned to pick up my sister, she was more than a little unhappy. She let me know her feelings. Overall, we enjoyed each other's company and still do.

Beverly and I attended the Perry School, which was a one-room country school a mile from our farm. My parents started me in first grade when I was four years old, because my sister was in the second grade and needed a companion to walk with to school. Our pet German shepherd, Rex, would walk with us, go home, and come back to pick us up at the end of the day. I remember some snowy days when I could step on the top of telephone poles. The drifts might have been from the snowplow, but whatever, they were very high. At the end of the year, the teacher and my parents decided it would be best if I repeated first grade so I could be in class with students my age. As it turned out, it was the right decision for me.

After I completed first grade, my parents moved to a farm in Utica proper and directly across the road from a two-room school. Grades one through four were in one room, and five through eight were in the other. Class sizes were small. We had seven in mine. I was the only boy with six girls during all eight grades.

Even though I was outnumbered, we played touch football and pom-pom pull-away. We are still good friends even though we ended up living in different parts of the country.

After grade school, Beverly and I attended St. Charles High School, which was larger, with thirty to forty classmates. I played football, basketball, track, and baseball. There were forty-two students in my 1949 graduating class. Today, twenty-five classmates are living, and we meet every year to visit, eat, and talk over old times.

Before and after school, my dad and I milked thirty-two cows by hand, usually dividing the herd with sixteen cows each. A good memory was squirting milk from the cow to my pet cat sitting nearby, who would not spill a drop of the stream of milk coming her way. The cat never went hungry.

My responsibility on the farm, besides normal chores, was getting the cattle from the fields and herding them to the barn for milking. I would feed them every morning and night, staring right into their faces. Sometimes their faces would remind me of people. One time, when I was eight or nine years old, I was walking downtown in Utica and met Mrs. Stupey, a widow. I looked her in the eye and said, "We have a cow at home that looks just like you." I meant that to be a compliment, but she did not take it that way. Word got back to my mother, and she made it very clear that it wasn't the proper thing to say no matter how much I might have loved the cow.

Sometime between the ages of twelve to fourteen, my father finally purchased a DeLaVal milking machine, which was very helpful. But we still had to put the machine on the udder and put the milk away. Naturally, doing chores meant missing many afternoons of fun with my classmates and friends at the park.

Over the years, I had various experiences on the farm, such as haying, threshing, bundling grain, and filling the silo with chopped corn. Duties also included helping with cows, horses, sheep, and chickens. I was in a 4-H club and raised baby steers and lambs to adulthood to show at the local fair. The animals would become pets because of all the hard work training them for show. The animals would become very good friends and would follow me around without a rope. Thursday was judging day, and you would get a white, red, or purple ribbon for the quality of your animal and how they behaved. You always wanted the purple ribbon for your animal, but they had to be outstanding to achieve that

ribbon. Friday was the dreaded day for 4-H participants at the fair: an auction was held to sell the animals. That was always a sad day— lots of tears.

As I look back, this was a great way to grow up and learn a solid work ethic. I did take part in sports, and my father would let me know if I got home late for chores. Yet he never missed a game. Upon graduation from high school, my father asked if I was interested in staying on the farm or if I would like to continue with school. I asked my father if he was keeping the milk cows or if he had considered selling them for beef cattle. He stated that he was keeping the dairy cattle, and I remarked that I would be going to school. He understood.

I feel that farming gave me the background to be sensitive to all feelings, whether it be a child, student, parent, animal, and—yes—even plants. Being sensitive is most important in helping me understand another person for appearance, attitude, behavior, sexual orientation, religion, or mental capacity before judging. To each his own, as long as it is not harming others. Independence makes the world exciting. Animals that are domesticated can't take care of themselves, so it is the responsibility of the caretaker to feed and care for them on a regular basis. Garden plants need care in their growth to produce the highest yield and be strong and healthy.

Preparation to take on life's work takes many avenues. My part-time jobs were useful and varied. While in college, I worked a night shift at Boland's plastic factory, making light raincoats. At Schuler Cherry Hump factory, I helped make delicious chocolate cherry hump candies. A college buddy and I decided to earn extra money by skinning mink at a mink farm. I would go to my friend Mary's dormitory for dinner. She did not appreciate my company much because I had the mink smell; it is like skunk.

In the summer months, I was a gandy dancer—a railroad worker—putting down new rails and driving spikes. All this heavy work was for leveling track so train passengers could have a smooth ride. During Christmas vacations, I was a US Postal Service mailman, delivering mail house to house.

For two summers, I drove an old, beat-up dump truck, delivering large rocks that were dynamited out of a side hill in a stone-quarry and loaded onto my truck with a Caterpillar. I would drive these big boulders to a rock crusher and dump in the load. The crusher would break them up and make what is called crushed rock. Other dump trucks would take the crushed rock and spread it on roadways. I wanted to drive the nicer trucks on the road and, finally, I got the opportunity, which was much more fun. I do remember a warning that if the brakes went out on the truck with a full load of gravel, get out before the truck hits something solid because the force of the gravel would crush you.

Driving a truck with no windows, no doors, and a ripped-up seat was not like driving a luxury truck with a radio for communicating back and forth in the quarry. I looked for something to break the monotony. The summer days were all warm. I had to cross a creek every time I drove from the quarry to the crusher. During lunchtime, I noticed that the head mechanic always sat on an old Caterpillar seat on the garage floor directly under a stovepipe used for venting the potbellied stove—for heating on cold days, but it was removed for the summer. The mechanic was not known for his humor and didn't like it much when a driver brought in a truck for repair. As an eighteen-year-old, I could not resist going to the creek with a five-gallon pail, filling it with water, climbing quietly upon the roof, and dumping the whole pail of water down the stovepipe. When I came down and went into the shed, there he stood, soaking wet with the soot from the pipe all over him. When he saw me, and realized I was the culprit, he came after me. I took off running as fast as I could through the quarry. I knew what would happen if he caught me. Fortunately, I was younger and faster, and he finally tired. The rest of the crew thought the prank was funny, but they wouldn't admit it. Finally, when we got back to the shed, he just looked at me but didn't attack. I apologized later and he accepted.

I was not alone in pulling pranks. The man running the Caterpillar loading shovel did some nasty things also. I would drive to the quarry with the doorless and windowless truck after a rain, park the truck, and wait to be loaded. The operator would pick up the largest, flattest rock, raise it as high as he could with his shovel, and then drop it in a puddle of water next to the truck. The splash would just about wash me out of my seat. The pranks did make the days go by a little faster, especially when doing such a tedious job.

After I started teaching, the teachers were always looking for ways to make extra money. I worked at Hopkins Post Office during Christmas, delivering mail door to door: a tough job when the temperature dropped to twenty below zero. Raising chinchillas and selling Shaklee products was another attempt at earning a little more money to support a growing family. In the summer, I worked as a carpenter and helped build the home we live in now. I also put in curbs and gutters for two summers before my time became more committed to administrator's duties. I am happy I had a variety of jobs. The experiences gave me many skills in areas I would not have known otherwise. I met individuals making good livings with those jobs, but I knew I didn't want to do those things for the rest of my life.

. . . .

Chapter 2

College and the Army Years

Now was the time for me to move on. I had an invitation with a working scholarship to attend Winona State Teachers College and play football and run track. The work was basically picking up towels that were left lying around the locker room and doing some cleanup. I accepted the invitation and went to early football practice prior to the start of school. When the first practice came, I weighed in at most 150 pounds. As I entered the locker room and looked around at the 250-pound World War II veterans, I thought, *what am I doing here?* As it turned out, I did all right as a running back and a safety for three seasons. My third year of football was cut short when a good friend, Harry Buck, tackled me when I was in the air, throwing a pass. I braced my fall with my arm and dislocated and broke my left elbow.

One of the experiences I remember from football at Winona was during a game with Bemidji State College. I had broken my front tooth two years before, and I was fitted with a partial plate with one tooth on it. It was fine unless I said something that forced air through it; then the plate would become loose.

During this particular time, I was playing running back, and my friend Dick Kowles was a wide receiver. One day, he caught a pass and was running for a touchdown; I was running behind to block when a defender was getting close, and I yelled, "Cut." With that word, my tooth went flying. This was prior to wearing mouth guards. I would have liked a picture of the ensuing activity. The game was stopped, and both teams were on our hands and knees, searching for the tooth. One of the Bemidji players found it in the white marking line. He gave it to me, I rinsed it off, put it back in my mouth, and the game resumed. I don't even remember who won the game.

The Military

The Korean War broke out, and I was drafted into the US Army in 1952 after my junior year of college. I considered asking for a deferment, but most of my friends were already in the military. I thought the government could draft me, and they did, for a two-year period. I was sent to Camp Sheridan, Illinois, to be inducted and assigned to sixteen weeks of basic training at Fort Bliss, El Paso, Texas. August in a hot desert area with the white-sand proving ground nearby meant very hot temperatures. Trainees had twenty-four-mile forced marches with very little water. We were not allowed to wear sunglasses even while training in the bright white sand. Part of the training, I guess, was to take orders and learn to tough it out.

The first eight weeks of basic was infantry training. The second eight weeks was training with heavy 90-mm guns and mortars. On the last day of basic training, our permanent assignments were posted. Everyone was nervous because the Korean War had begun. The company was split into three sections: those sent to Los Angeles for embarking were going to Korea; those sent to Camp Kilmer, New Brunswick, New Jersey, were going to Germany; and the other third were assigned to various camps within the United States.

I was sent to Camp Kilmer, New Brunswick, New Jersey, where eventually our unit embarked on a troop ship to Bremen, Germany, and then by train to Gelnhausen, Germany. We became part of the 12th infantry regiment, located sixteen kilometers north of Frankfurt.

My role on the troop ship was to clean and mop the latrines. Before I left for Camp Kilmer, my local pharmacist  gave me some pills that would help avoid seasickness. The pills worked for me, so I was assigned that unenviable job. It was not pleasant because 90 percent of the troops were very seasick all the way from New York to Bremen. Once we arrived at Gelnhausen, I was assigned to the fire direction center for 4.2 mortars.

I was honorably discharged as a sergeant in June 1954, and returned to finish my final year at Winona State Teachers College, graduating in June 1955.

My majors and minor in college were the following: science, industrial arts, coaching, and physical education. My mentors for choosing these fields were my high school teacher Mr. Doug Delano, industrial arts, physical education, and coaching; Mr. Joe Karakas, science; and my high school principal Don Coppins, administration.

Chapter 3

The Most Important Day of My Life

After high school, I went to college in the fall of 1949, enrolling at Winona State. I was successful in college, meaning that I passed all the subjects in which I was enrolled.

During my sophomore year, I was taking an 8:00 a.m. Earth Science class from Dr. Seitz. The class had started, and Dr. Seitz had begun his lecture when in walked this young female student.

The professor stated, "Miss Kilkelly, you're late again!" My attention went immediately to this young woman. As the lecture resumed, my mind was saying over and over that she had such a cute name and was nice looking besides. I had to meet her and get to know her.

That evening, I was at the local college hangout playing rap poker with friends. The bet: if you lose, you drink a glass of beer with a raw egg. I lost, so I was standing at the bar drinking this glass of beer with a raw egg in it. Watching all this was someone who I seriously wanted to meet. I later learned that she just dropped in to the Milwaukee Bar, the college hangout, after a Catholic Newman Club meeting.

After the activity was over, I approached her and asked whether she would like a chaperone back to the dormitory. She was reluctant at first, but spoke with friends who said I wasn't a bad sort. The walk went well, and I asked to go out with her later on. She said okay and our first formal date was on St. Patrick's Day, 1951. We dated all year until I was drafted into the army.

She was with me on the bus when I went to St. Paul to be inducted into the army for two years. It was a sad day, but we felt our attraction to each other would last.

We corresponded regularly once I reached Germany. Over time, we even considered getting married by telephone. We didn't know if that was possible, but we talked about it anyway.

When I was discharged, I caught a train to Winona. She was there to meet me, and we both were so excited to see each other. We felt even closer than before, because we had kept in touch the whole time I was away.

After a short while, I decided that she was the one from whom I wanted to sit across the breakfast table every morning. I bought a diamond engagement ring for her. In my hometown, a small farming community of three thousand, the story is that I was so excited, I showed the ring to everyone in town before asking Mary for her hand.

I proposed to Mary on the shore of Lake Winona and gave her the ring. This was scary because I didn't know if she would say yes and accept the ring. Fortunately, she said yes.

We drove to Bayport, her hometown, so I could ask her father for her hand. It was a little later in the evening when we arrived at the Kilkelly residence in Bayport. He knew me because I dated her the year before I went into the service.

I thought he kind of liked me, but when I asked to marry Mary, he fell off the arm of the chair he was sitting on. He asked when, and I said next summer, a year away, in June, after I graduated. He said, "So soon?" Then he consented.

Mary and I were married June 10, 1955, on a Friday. We did that so we could have a short honeymoon before I had to return to Winona State to finish my final credits the following Monday.

Mary was fussy about not having the car all decked out with cans. She warned me ahead of time, but as we left the reception that afternoon, we said our good-byes and got in the car to leave, and  the car wouldn't go. I asked the best man, my very good friend, to keep an eye out for saboteurs. I trusted him. After everyone got a big laugh, my friend took the car off the blocks. Finally, Mary and  I bid farewell with cans clanging all along behind us. I looked in the rearview mirror and saw my grandfather laughing away; I found out later he was responsible. The first stop was the dump to untie the cans. The second stop was a little motel on the way to St.  Paul called the Sky Blue Waters. I preordered flowers for the room: our first night of marriage.

June 10, 1955: a most important day in my life, and our wedding anniversary. We have lived together as man and wife for over sixty-one years. We have five wonderful adult children.

Chapter 4

First Teaching Jobs

After serving in the army, I still had a year to finish my requirements for graduation. Upon my graduation and our marriage on June 10, 1955, we wanted to find teaching jobs together. We were just a very young, happy, newly married couple looking for teacher employment somewhere. One morning as we were leaving campus to drive to Wadena for an interview, the placement director yelled out the window, saying there was an opening for a first-grade teacher and a high school industrial arts teacher at Eden Prairie, Minnesota.

We said we must look at a map to see where that city was located. We looked but couldn't find an Eden Prairie. Mary's brother flew small airplanes from the Lake Elmo Airport to Eden Prairie's Flying Cloud Airport. He told us in general how to get there from Winona. Think back to 1955. Freeway 494 did not exist, nor was there much in Bloomington. The only road to Eden Prairie was a two-lane road called 78th Street. We took that and soon came upon a Mobile gas station that had a big red-and-white horse sign on top.

We were getting into the country; we thought we had better stop and ask if they knew where Eden Prairie was. So we pulled into the station. This polite gentleman looked at us and said, "This is it." We

17

looked around and didn't see much of anything beyond the station. We mentioned that we were there to interview for teaching jobs at the Eden Prairie schools. He kindly gave us directions to the school. It wasn't easy because all the roads were gravel and there was not one stop sign in the whole township. The gentleman who had helped us was a legend himself, Mr. Jessie Schwartz Sr., a famous local baseball player who was the operator of the Flying Red Horse filling station and restaurant. This was a popular stopping place for individuals coming to Minneapolis from the south or west. Mr. Schwartz later served on the school board. Mary and I found the two-story school building sitting on a hill overlooking a pretty lake.

We interviewed for some time with Mr. Huls, the superintendent. Following the interview, he offered both of us contracts to teach at Eden Prairie. We had talked about the situation on the drive there and agreed that even though it was small now, we were sure the area would grow. We thought that it would be fun to be a part of a new community and to grow with it. Even though the salary was not the best, both of us were very excited to be a part of Eden Prairie.

At the time, Eden Prairie was a township, but we knew being that close to Minneapolis, surrounded by Minnetonka on the north, Edina and Bloomington on the east, and the Minnesota River on the south, that there was no way it would not grow. In 1955, there were less than a thousand residents in the thirty-six square miles of Eden Prairie Township. For the most part, Eden Prairie was dairy farms and berry farms. There was no downtown and no major businesses, except Metropolitan Flying Cloud Airport and Northrup King.

Later, Mary and I heard that even though the school board approved our contract, there was some question about hiring a husband and wife team. There was another factor. I had converted to Catholicism to join my wife in religion when we married. Now there would be two more Catholics. Prior to our marriage, I had different faiths. Whichever church was closest to our farm was the one my parents joined. Mary had been born and raised Catholic. Nothing came of this concern, and we were graciously accepted by the total faculty of fifteen for grades one through twelve. The board members were Calvin Anderson, Ernie Hone, and Harry Picha.

The contracts for the 1955–56 school year were for Mary to teach first grade and for me to teach industrial arts to grades seven through twelve, to assist coaching basketball  during the week, and to teach adult education classes in the evening for six-week periods. There were some other duties outlined by the principal. Teachers were required to attend all PTA (Parent Teacher Association) meetings. Male faculty were required to get bus drivers' licenses, because the district only had four drivers and they served as custodians during the day.

Mary's first contract was twenty-four hundred dollars yearly. Mine was thirty-two hundred plus seventy-five dollars for coaching, which included ninth-grade basketball on Saturdays and assistant  coaching during the week. Teachers were paid monthly. If you wanted food on the table at the end of the month, it was necessary to watch the spending closely.

Once our contracts were offered, we needed a place to stay for the year. Mary did not know how to drive at the time, so we looked for something close so I could shuttle her home before my afternoon activities. We were told about Pidcock Apartments a half mile down the road. We visited Mrs. Pidcock, and fortunately for us, she had a vacancy. She rented the one-bedroom furnished unit to us for seventy-five dollars per month. In the same building, there were four upper-level units. They were all occupied with Eden Prairie teachers. How lucky could a couple be?

We were so excited: a new home, and each of us had a contract to teach in a new, growing community. The area was small in population but so close to the Twin Cities, we couldn't believe our good fortune. Newly married, military time completed, and we found a place we loved with friendly and helpful people. The township was small enough that we got to know most everyone living there.

That afternoon, we explored Eden Prairie. The first stop was the lookout by Flying Cloud Airport, south of old 169, to look down on the Minnesota River Valley and the surrounding lakes. The views of the Minnesota River were spectacular. We drove by the beautiful lakes in Eden Prairie. The largest were Riley, Bryant, Duck, Round, Anderson, and Starring.

We drove past Cedar Hills Golf Club and ski area. At the top of the hill was a beautiful view of the river valley. The views were the same driving south on Dell Road. The roadways had many roadside vegetable stands, with owner's names like Kopesky, Holasek, Peterson, Raguet, and Kerbers. The countryside had many dairy and grain farms, with family names of Bren, Nesbitt, Miller, Shutrop, Kerber, Jacques, Mitchell, Boyd, Brekke, Brown, Kopesky, and Anderson.

There was a dance hall by Riley Lake called Dutch's Resort, which was a busy place, I had been told. On Friday nights, there was entertainment with a band or singers. No real grocery stores or restaurants could be found. There was Lions Tap, but teachers were not allowed there because beer was served. After work, sometimes Mary and I would go to Pauley's Bar in Chanhassen, joining other teachers from Chaska, Shakopee, Minnetonka, and Waconia to exchange ideas. We knew faculty members in all the neighboring schools. Many teachers were World War II and Korean veterans, enjoying their newfound life. They were all good, hardworking, conscientious teachers. The motto at the time was "Work hard, play hard."

Eden Prairie was an unincorporated township until 1963, when it became a village. In 1974, it became a city. Once it became a village, there was a mayor and city council. The average age of the population in Eden Prairie when it became a city was thirty-seven. The

Metro Area Planning Commission for land use was instrumental in designing parks, residential, and commercial areas. The commission did a good job with green spaces in the city, which today makes it a good place to live.

In the early days, as mentioned before, Eden Prairie was built around berry and dairy farms. Northrup King had land on the northwest corner of old Highway 169 and Anderson Lakes Parkway. The company had many acres of beautiful flowers and varieties of hybrid corn. Students worked for the company detasseling corn and weeding.

Businesses began, sewer and water lines were installed, and there were building codes. A village hall was built.

People from Minneapolis thought Eden Prairie was really in the sticks. We didn't feel that way because this was home to us. As time passed, their impression changed.

Growth was expected, but at first, it was slow. Today the city's population is over sixty-two thousand. Eden Prairie has grown from one school encompassing all grades to one large high school, six elementary schools, and a middle school for grades six through eight. In 1955, the district had seventeen teachers and three hundred students in grades one through twelve. An International School is based in Eden Prairie, and two other private schools are located in the city.

In July 1955, the population of the Eden Prairie schools was all white, until 1982 when one student of color was enrolled. Now the school district is very diversified, with forty-eight languages spoken and many countries represented. I mention this to show the growth and change we were privileged to experience.

We were excited and could hardly wait to visit the school. There was a two-story brick building with a recent attachment, called the sheep shed; it was a one-level, long building attached to the main building. The superintendent and principal had their offices in the sheep shed, and all six grades of the high school had their classrooms in the one-level building. The four school buses were stored in the garage on the bottom floor. Elementary students' classrooms were on the upper floor of the two-story building.

The outside grounds were a mess, with tall grass and weeds around the backside of the school. My parents were invited to come to see our new place of employment. My mother looked and walked around and said, "We spent all that money for college and this is where you are going to work?" She obviously did not see what we saw in the potential. Eden Prairie is now the second largest school district in the state of Minnesota. Mother finally understood our excitement and was also proud.

We got settled in our apartment. Everything both of us owned was carried in our first car, a 1946 Ford. It was sold to us by my father's friend. Unfortunately, neither Dad nor I knew that the engine had a cracked block. When we drove from Winona to our apartment in Eden Prairie, we had to stop frequently to put water in the radiator.

The next step was my first teacher workshop. Mary taught in Stillwater while I was in the military, serving in Germany. She was experienced; I wasn't. The workshop was a week before the start of school. Both of us were anxious to meet the rest of the teaching staff and find out our assignments and the rest of the rules of operation. After breakfast in our new apartment, we went to our new school for work.

Superintendent Huls introduced us to the other fifteen teachers in District 272.

1955–56 Faculty. Front Row: Mrs. Simons, Mrs. Connaughty, Mrs. Hall, Mrs. Walker, Mrs. Erkilla, Mrs. Wanek, Mrs. Bartlett, Miss Ware, Miss Nye
Second Row: Mr. Connaughty, Mr. Hulls, Mrs. Saxon, Mrs. Axelson, Mrs. McReavye, Miss Urbashich, Mrs. Oleson, Mr. Engstrom, Mr. Nelson

There were four men on the staff. Mr. Conley Engstrom was the science teacher. The superintendent taught classes, and principal Nelson taught classes. I was given the industrial arts assignment. During the four days of the workshop, we were informed about the community, the regulations of the school, and our expectations as teachers. We had time to prepare our rooms and lessons for the first day of school. I was the only rookie teacher in the bunch and probably the most nervous one.

I was young, energetic, and willing to take on any responsibility. Mary and I were the newcomers to a small, experienced staff who had been together for some time. I have been told that we, as outsiders, brought in some excitement and fresh ideas to Eden Prairie, not knowing the old traditions. Eden Prairie was a small community; everyone knew everyone else.

Following the week of the workshop, the opening day of school was Monday. I was really excited to meet the students, but I was also full of anxiety. *Will the students accept me? Will they listen? Will I do the right thing? Will my lessons sound exciting or at least good to them?*

At 7:30 a.m., the students started walking into school. All the teachers were standing at their classroom doors to welcome them for the new school year. I was standing by the door to the industrial arts classroom. Being young-looking and only six years older than the seniors, I wondered if the students would think, "Who is this guy?"

The first day was very exciting, with the opportunity to actually meet the youngsters from seventh grade through twelfth: six classes out of the seven-hour day. Grades seven and eight were combined. A teacher's seventh hour was supervising a study hall.

Experience has taught me that the first day of school is not necessarily an indication of what the rest of the school year behavior will be like. Students are new to the faculty after a long vacation. Teachers are new to them. They do not know the rules of the teacher or the quality. Class time is a get-acquainted day for both student and teacher. Ninety-nine percent of the students look forward to the first day. There is that very small percentage that is looking for the little weak spot in the teacher for testing that person's skill. At the same time, the teacher is evaluating students, trying to find out which ones are sincere and which are the ones who are testing. The decisions of both are not necessarily permanent decisions. Much depends on the skill of the teacher to impress students with the subject matter and caring attitude. The first judgment is not always the right one in either case.

As a new teacher, the students tested me many times. I enjoyed the challenge and had confidence that I could handle anything they wanted to do. One of those circumstances was when someone in class put a thumbtack on my chair. I remembered my teaching theory class about not overreacting. Without knowing it was there, I sat down and immediately knew what was on the chair, but I didn't react in any way; I just sat there and looked around the room. Soon students started looking at the culprit to find out a reaction. They found the individual for me. He and I had a meeting after school. We talked it over and both agreed the incident was not appreciated. It never happened again.

Other incidents happened that first year that would upset me, so I would wake up at night and write notes about making new student rules. The next day, students would greet me with a smile and say,

"Good morning, Mr. Connaughty." I would take my notes out and tear them up and smile back at them.

Another incident that first year was with the senior industrial arts class. They made it popular in the colder months to wear gloves. One day they came to class with gloves on and refused to take them off. I said they could not work with the machines wearing their gloves. Instead of taking the gloves off, they just sat on their stools. I decided not to fight the situation. I went to my adjoining office and let them sit. A short time later, I noticed one of the boys took off his gloves and put them on the bench. Soon others did the same. They looked at me, and I came out of the office as the students started working on their projects. Someone must have realized that I was the one who handed out the grades.

I loved teaching: the kids and the challenges. To have a wife who also had experiences in teaching helped me greatly. Mary was a great teacher with the qualities that were necessary, such as patience, understanding, knowledge, and diagnostic skills. She would explain that I either did the right thing or recommend a better way I could have handled it. Even with her good advice, I lost twenty pounds that first year of teaching.

There were thirteen students in that first graduating class of 1956. The previous year there were twelve graduates.

At the end of the school year, I visited with the superintendent and told him that maybe teaching wasn't for me and that I would look for another profession. He said, "Don't you even think of that!" He complimented me on my energy and caring attitude in dealing with the students. "You are doing just fine, and this is what you should be doing." Thank you, Mr. Huls.

After that first year, I realized what the responsibility of a teacher entailed:

- Acting as parent, counselor, and psychologist during the day
- Using discipline and praise properly
- Welcoming students every morning with a smile, regardless of their interest in being there

- Serving as doctor—removing slivers, washing and bandaging abrasions, stopping bloody noses
- Preventing bullying between boys or girls
- Having an atmosphere in the classroom so students will be excited about learning
- Chaperoning dances, proms, etc.
- Teaching

Further education was a self-expectation. I attended the University of Minnesota during the summers to achieve my master's and a specialist degree in administration.

I also learned about negotiating teacher contracts at that time. All seventeen members of the teaching staff were in one building, and we wanted to talk contract for the following year. All of us joined the MFT (Minnesota Federation of Teachers) so we could be stronger for negotiations. We had a presentation asking for a small raise. The school board came back with their own offer of a seventy-five dollar raise for the year: take it or leave it. As I recall, everyone accepted their new contract offer for 1956–57. Back to MEA (Minnesota Education Association).

The first two years I taught industrial arts. Working evenings and weekends, I built the Home Economics cabinets in the sheep shed addition. The beautiful birch wood cabinets are still there. The tool racks in industrial arts were rebuilt at the same time. Before I became the teacher, evidently students were given permission to build knives in metal class. Unfortunately, some used the tool cabinet as a target for their knives. The cabinets were a chopped-up mess. I built new tool racks on the weekend. The students who did that must have graduated before I came because it didn't seem we had anyone in class who would be that destructive.

While walking down the hall one morning, I noticed Mike carrying a long shotgun. "What do you plan on doing with that gun?" I asked. Mike stated that a lot of the boys brought their guns to school so they could go hunting after school. "What do you do with them until then?" I asked.

Mike said, "We put them in our lockers." That sounded reasonable to me. No harm was done, and nothing was thought about it again. The boys also needed knives so they could clean the game they shot. The knives were either put in the lockers or kept in their pants pockets. At the time, it was a harmless thing for them. They were not talked about during the day, and after school, they took them out of their lockers and went looking for game. The next morning, Mike brought me a nice cleaned pheasant.

Following my first two years of teaching full-time industrial arts, I was given the opportunity to teach biology and physical education. I enjoyed industrial arts, but biology was a second major for me that I wanted to teach. The third year, I taught both industrial arts and biology and eventually replaced industrial arts with physical education. As an example of the size of a grade, here is one year where the whole grade fit in or on one car.

I had written an autobiography for an English class assignment during my sophomore year in high school. My mother, who read most of my compositions, later pointed out that I had accomplished all the things I had written about while working at the Eden Prairie Schools.

A Pleasant Diversion with Sadness

During the summer following my first year of teaching, I worked for a carpenter, Mr. Unze, as his helper. My wife Mary and I knew that she was having a baby, due sometime in August 1956. I had cut my finger with a hatchet at work and had to go to the hospital for stitches. I was supposed to pick up milk and eggs at the store on June 15 before coming home. I did, and as I walked into the house, Mary exclaimed, "I think the baby is coming. We have to go to the hospital right away." With that greeting, I dropped the eggs and milk on the floor. You can guess the mess that left. I scrambled and cleaned what I could, and Mary was all packed to go. She was dressed nicely so if it was a false alarm, we could go to a movie.

We jumped into the car, and down to St. Francis Hospital in Shakopee we went. We were on the steps when Dr. Pearson walked out and said, "Why are you two here?" and Mary said, "I think I am ready to deliver the baby." He said, "All mothers with their first child think they are delivering early, but come in. We will check you out." Soon the doctor sent her to the delivery room and sent me to the waiting room. He said, "We will notify you about what is happening."

Many hours later, a Catholic sister nurse came into the waiting room and said, "You have a little girl, but she is very small." A short time later, she came back and said, "You have another daughter, but again, very small." They were seven weeks premature and weighed in at three pounds each. They were identical twin girls, whom we named Ellen Mary and Patricia Mary. We had no idea Mary would deliver twins. They were very tiny; unfortunately, Patricia's lungs were not developed enough for her to survive. Ellen was put in an isolette for thirty days for her to get big enough and strong enough to go home. She survived but thinks of her sister often. That is the beginning of our family, born June 16, 1956.

We decided that we should maybe look for at least a two-bedroom home. We were fortunate to find a home for rent on Glen Lake. It was a two-bedroom with a screened porch and nice yard that went to the lake. Rent was seventy-five dollars per month. The property was owned by Joe Tolasek, a garage owner on Excelsior Boulevard in Glen Lake. Our second living child was born there on September 1, 1957, and was named Julia Ann.

We lived there for two years before purchasing our first home. Ecklund Swedlund was the builder. The prices of his three models were $15,400, $15,900, and $16,400. We selected the middle-priced home, which was in a brand-new area on a hill. The house had three bedrooms, a bath, two fireplaces, and a tuck-under garage. The prices demonstrate the housing market in the early 1960s. Two years later, we built our present home.

Chapter 5

The Early Football and Track Years

I played football and participated in track for four years in high school and three years at Winona State. I also played football for a year while in the army in Germany, where I injured my knee badly enough to end my career with contact sports and hurdling in track.

Mr. Conley Engstrom was the athletic director at Eden Prairie. He taught science and math and coached basketball and baseball.

First Row: D. Ravnholdt, J. Roeser, B. Roaderick, D. Schmidt, G. Stodola, B. Pauly, B. Roaderick
Second Row: Mr. Engstrom, R. Wigley, D. Larson, S. Roe, M. Susemihl, B. Brekke, B. Wittenberg, Mr. Connaughty

He was successful in all areas, a much-loved teacher and coach. I was his assistant and coached the B team.

First Row: W. Moran, T. Roeser, D. Hirt, K. Kearney, G. Stodola, P. Anderson, J. Geiger

Second Row: Mr. Connaughty, L. Nesbitt, D. Larson, D. Kormylo, D. Ravnholdt, B. Roaderick, B. Roaderick, Mr. Engstrom

On Saturdays, I coached the ninth graders, called the C-squad.

First Row: S. Quam, T. Eames, S. Peterson, C. Croissant, T. Chevalier, B. Wittenberg

Second Row: Mr. Connaughty, R. Marsh, A. Dressen, B. Beggs, W. Eggan, L. Woodward, Mr. Engstrom

During my second year, I asked if we might start a football program. He said we could check out the cost of equipment and present it to the school board. We did and set up a meeting with the superintendent and school board to present a proposal to start a football program.

Most members of the school board were farmers, and when we said practices would begin two weeks prior to the start of school, they questioned the feasibility of that since they needed the boys to help with harvesting. Conley and I talked about the benefits and the fact that the school was growing. Playing nine-man football was considered, but schools that played nine-man were good distances away. Both of us stressed that eleven-man was what we wanted to play. The board agreed, and football joined the sports program of basketball, baseball, and cheerleading at Eden Prairie High School.

Conley and I got bids for equipment and uniforms for the following fall. We spoke to many vendors but decided on A & B Sporting Goods in Minneapolis to furnish our first equipment and uniforms. Red-and-black uniforms—white for home games—were our colors. That summer, I built cabinets in the boys' locker room in the main building to store the pads and uniforms. We were ready for our first season of football in 1957.

The first year we learned football fundamentals. The boys did a lot of scrimmaging with teams from the Hennepin County Boys Home, state champions Washburn, and Richfield.

First Row: J. Shidla, D. Nesbitt, L. Woodward, B. Menge, J. Fagerstrom, J. Kennedy, M. Gay, J. Holasek
Second Row: R. Ravnholdt, M. Torgerson, J. Ackerman, W. Moran, T. Roser, L. Berquist, D. Pomerleau, A. Kramer, D. Schmidt, K. Kopesky

Third Row: Mr. Connaughty, T. Thompson, L. Nesbitt, P. Anderson, B. Roaderick, G. Stodala, B. Ciskobsky, B. Roaderick, D. Ravnholdt, Mr. Engstrom

Fourth Row: W. Tobias, D. Larson, A. Hjorth, D. Larson, S. Roe, D. Kormylo, R. Wigley, B. Pauly, G. Koskela

Our team learned a lot from the opposing players. Their coaches were gracious and helpful. Most of our players had never seen a football game, let alone played the game. They were busy on the farm. Most of their parents had never seen a football game either. There was no television in Eden Prairie at this time.

Conley Engstrom was my first assistant coach. We worked very hard, as did the players. We were preparing for the next year, when we would be playing in a full-sized conference with schools that had been playing football for years. We wanted our players to know the fundamentals of blocking and tackling. To make them strong and ready to take hits, we had them run the hill just west of the school. The custodian of the grounds didn't appreciate it much because he was always trying to grow nice grass on that hill, and the cleats on the football shoes did more than aerate grass.

Besides showing the boys how the pads fit and how they were worn, it was necessary to alleviate the anxiety of mothers. They were worried about the contact sports. I had meetings with mothers to show the protection the boys had while wearing all the pads. A couple of the players were models and would dress with the pads, and I would explain what each pad protected. The mothers left feeling a little more at ease.

A football field was needed for practices even though the first year was game-like scrimmages for teaching and learning.

I checked with the custodians—only four—to see if they could help with making a field. They were reluctant because they had their hands full preparing the school and grounds for the upcoming school year.

Mr. Joe Shidla helped, and we laid out a field just north of the sheep shed extension. The field was grass but had a steep eight-foot drop at the far end. So the field was official in width, but only eighty yards in length. I made goal posts out of 2 x 4s, placing them at the end toward the sheep shed building. If a player scored on the far end of the field, it was necessary to go to the other end to kick an extra point. That lasted one year.

The Eden Prairie school was a member of the Minnesota Valley Conference, which included Chaska, Shakopee, Waconia, Watertown, Orono, University High, Norwood Young America, and for a short time, Burnsville. For the first regular season, we did not have a legal field of our own. The team played on opposing teams' fields. We even played one game at a park in Minneapolis.

The first regular conference game was against Shakopee, on their field. They were the victor. The game was delayed while our team waited for our game uniforms to arrive from the sporting goods agent. A half hour after the scheduled starting time, the uniforms were delivered. Every player had to make the complete change in the bus. With their new red-and-black uniforms, the team ran onto the field to a rousing cheer from everyone at the game.

First Row: M. Geiger, D. Nesbitt, B. Menge, J. Holsek, D. Schmidt, A. Kramer, W. Moran, P. Anderson, G. Thompson

Second Row: D. Pomerleau, T. Roeser, J. Pauly, L. Berquist, L. Nesbitt, R. Ravnholdt, D. Ravnholdt, B. Pauly, W. Tobias

Third Row: Mr. Connaughty, B. Ciskovsky, J. Linner, D. Larson, R. Wigley, D. Kormylo, D. Larson, S. Roe, A. Hjorth

Here's one example of how new football was to Eden Prairie. Before one game, one mother called my wife and said John would not be coming to the game because it was raining outside—not storming—just raining. John was a starter for the team, so he had to be replaced from a limited number of substitutes.

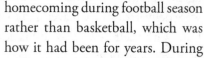

The fall of 1959 was the historic first football victory for the Eden Prairie Eagles against Golden Valley. James Christianson was the assistant coach during that first win. I have the game football with the names of all players, manager, and assistant coach.

After that game, the coaches decided it was time to have homecoming during football season rather than basketball, which was how it had been for years. During the next season, the students gathered wood for a giant bonfire, with permission of Fire Chief Ray Mitchell. An afternoon parade and a homecoming dance became part of the annual celebration.

The most exciting game for me was the first time Eden Prairie beat Orono. Orono was coached by my high school coach, Mr. Pesonen. Our coaching staff always felt

that Orono had such big players, and so many, in comparison. I often made the comment that some of their players' thighs were bigger than our kids' waists. Eden Prairie won that game after being beaten the previous years. The feeling was special and felt so good.

In 1958, a teaching colleague, Fred Hagen, joined the staff in the business department. In 1959, he became the ninth grade football coach. His players got a good start in fundamental football. He coached for over twenty-five years.

Parents soon became interested in the football program. Two or three were encouraged to start a Little League for younger players. Parents organized and started Little League football for fifth and sixth graders in the early '60s. They raised money to buy equipment, storing the equipment in a building used by the Gun Club close to Round Lake. Other parents helped coach on early evenings. This was the beginning of helping children gain experience in the sport of football before they came to high school. As the program and school population grew, the practices for the league moved to fields at Flying Cloud Airport. The parents did a good job of preparing the players for high school football. Later in the fall, when it got dark, early, they would park their cars in a manner so they could shine the lights to illuminate the field.

After graduation, some football players played at Division II and III colleges throughout the country. A few played at Division I schools, including the University of Minnesota. One of Eden Prairie's earlier football players was on the varsity team at the University of Minnesota. George Adzick was recruited and played professionally for the Seattle Seahawks. He is now connected with a responsible position for the University of Minnesota Alumni Association. His brother Mark was also a fine athlete.

The Westerhaus family had six boys who were good student-athletes. Two played for the University of Minnesota. Another was a superintendent of schools.

When I was coaching, my football manager and track manager was very conscientious, and I felt the best. His life after college has made him a part of the University of Minnesota as a faithful supporter. He goes beyond being just a fan and knows many of the players in most of the sports the university offers. Throughout his life, he emphasized diligence and awareness in the sports world. He is more than a home spectator traveling afar to support the teams. Terry Hanna is an example of a dependable and trusting individual.

Eden Prairie has had five head football coaches from 1957 to 2016. From beginning to present: Curt Connaughty, John Ryski, Chuck Rogers, Tim Kasprowicz, and Mike Grant. My assistants during my coaching career were Engstrom, Christianson, Ryski, Leopold, Braatlund, Yore, Werpy. Usually only one assistant per season accept the last three years we had 2. Over the later twenty-year period, Grant has developed ten large school state championships and a very successful football program. Since 1955, the number of sports activities grew from two to thirty-three: fifteen for boys, and eighteen for girls. Eden Prairie has the largest extracurricular program for schools in the country, according to Activities Coordinator Mike Grant.

All early coaches, players, and parents take no credit for the current success that the Eagles are having. However, everyone is proud that they were involved at the beginning of the sport when Eden Prairie was a very small school.

Beginning Track

During the spring of 1958, the school board allowed me to start a boys' track program. We did not have a designated or regulation track. Track participants ran on the roads around the school and on the short football field. The track team traveled to meets via my old, green seven-passenger station wagon. I was the driver.

The Eden Prairie sports program was now football, basketball, track, baseball, and cheerleading.

First Row: D. Kopesky, R. Kopesky, D. Dredge, W. Boyd, M. Nelson, M. Anderson

Steve Roe, a 1959 Eden Prairie student-athlete, was a student at the University of Minnesota's Engineering Department. He came back to school one day, and I was talking to him about how nice it would be if we had a regular track for the team.

The next day, Steve came with all his survey equipment. The two of us laid out the first 440-yard track. We staked out the inside and outside perimeters. I then asked Mr. Johnson, the road-grader operator for the township, if he could grade between the stakes. A good man, he graded out about three feet of grass and dirt all around the track. That gave the track boys something to run on that was smooth. Now they could be timed, and the coach could know how fast they ran.

We asked an owner of a lumberyard in Bloomington, Mr. Eames, if he could provide lumber so we could put a curb around the track. I was working for a curb and gutter company during the summer, pouring and leveling concrete. I ordered a load of concrete for these areas and made the two slabs for throwing discus and shot put. We dug out landing pits for the long jump, high jump, and pole vault, and filled them with sand. We were ready now to invite other schools to compete against Eden Prairie at home on our own track.

This was Eden Prairie's first homemade track. Wouldn't you know, the following

Dorothy McIntyre starting a race.

39

year, the National Track Association changed the distance of 440-yard track event to a 400 meters event. We needed to shorten what we had graded the year before.

Two years later, a professional track and football field developer from North St. Paul built us a beautiful track and football field. The large schools in the lake conference wanted to use it during a week of rain because the field had such a great crown; the drainage was excellent. The new areas were nice, but no lights or bleachers were provided. We played afternoon games, and spectators stood alongside the field.

Two years later, lights and bleachers were installed. At the start of the game, we tried to turn the lights on and they didn't come on. We had the installer come; he was a local fellow, and he finally got them lit a half hour later. This was Eden Prairie's first game under lights with bleachers for fans. No more day games. To witness all of this was awesome.

A Disappointment in Track

We had a good track team but had never won a conference championship. The day before the conference meet, we were figuring out which member of our track team could score points. Walter Koenst beat everyone in the conference that spring. He ran the 100, 220, and 440, so we were sure that would be enough to win the meet. While warming up for the race, he pulled a hamstring bad enough that he could not compete. Unfortunately for all of us, we didn't win the championship.

Chapter 6

. . . .

Students and Experiences

As an assistant principal, one assignment was being the administrator who dealt with most of the student discipline. It is a challenging experience to try to get the students to change their behavior without harming their personalities or self-confidence. Sometimes it takes many encounters before they recognize their behavior is not getting them anyplace but trouble. There are those few who will not recognize that what they are doing is not appropriate for a particular situation. They are very few in numbers. The majority recognize inappropriateness and make the mistake only once. I expect growing youth to make errors in judgment because they are working at deciding what kind of a people they want to be. In doing so, they try things that they find are not comfortable. Sometimes they are seen when they are testing the wrong thing. Like life itself, there are rules to live by. When they are broken, usually there are consequences.

One day, it was a normal, quiet day at school when a rumbling noise came from the hall. I went into the hall to find a student driving his motorcycle through the front door, down the hall, to the other end of the building, and out that door. He was stopped by a custodian before he might have hit a student coming from the other hall. It was planned because he had students holding both doors open so he could get through fast. It was during class time, and the halls were empty of most students.

The '60s were a hot decade for schools as well as the rest of the country. There was much unrest, partly due to the Vietnam crisis and President Kennedy's assassination. Brother, senator, and presidential hopeful Robert Kennedy was assassinated as well. Robert brought hope to youth in these testy times, and when he died, some positive influence for the country was also destroyed.

Dr. King's assassination sent a powerful message to everyone, but more so to the black society. Rioting and destruction took place around the country. Robert Kennedy, prior to his assassination, said that he understood Dr. King's assassination because he too had a brother killed by a white man. As it turned out, days later, Kennedy was gunned down by a white man. All these things made the country ill.

Eden Prairie felt that restlessness. I remember walking in the doors of the school each morning, and you could just feel the tension, the restlessness. It was a tough time to teach, but the actions of young people during that decade made changes in our society. The student on the motorcycle was sent home to his parents for a couple of days so they too could let him know his stunt was inappropriate and dangerous. It was a tough lesson for the student because his parents decided to sell his bike.

One day I heard rumors that some students were upset because the school board had decided to cut Christmas vacation to one week instead of two. I had a teacher meeting that morning to notify the teachers that there might be a student walkout. I told them, "If there is, stand by the doors to let students know you don't approve, but in no case touch or try to stop them physically from walking out. Once they are all out, I will talk with the student leaders and find out the reason and tell them my expectations to go back to their classrooms." It so happened that day the superintendent was gone and the head principal was out of the building. I was the only administrator on duty.

Around 9:00 a.m., I heard a bell go off, and I went outside the office, and the students were going out the different doors. I looked down the hall, and the first person I saw walking out was our daughter Ellen.

Once all students were outside, I asked if I could meet with the leaders of the class. We talked about the seriousness of the action, and I wanted to know the reason so it could be discussed. Many of the students had no idea why they walked out other than that everyone else was doing the same thing. The walkout was very peaceful, and I told the leaders I would report to the superintendent, and he would relay the information to the board. I asked the leaders to have the students report back to their classrooms. They did, and no punishment was dealt out.

There has not been another one, and the students had their experience. They did not initiate the first walkout in the state. Other schools had done it before. I followed through with my end of the bargain by reporting it to the superintendent. The students got an explanation from the school board as to why vacation was cut. My daughter Ellen was not the instigator, but she had heard of the action beforehand. She did not say a word to me prior to the activity.

Having three daughters in the same school where I was an administrator made administrating a little more challenging. Students who were disciplined for some reason or another felt it their right to take out their frustration by harassing the girls, calling their father names, and stating what they were going to do. That part was difficult even though we talked about it at home during family meals or family meetings. Mary and I do feel the final outcome has made them stronger adults.

The other phase was that being a principal's kid made them say they wanted to fit into the crowd. So they did, which resulted in my having to suspend two of our three girls for breaking school rules. Their mother would have to bring them back after they served their time, and they would meet with the other principal to get back to school. Discussions at home were pretty heavy as well. Overall, the girls did enjoy their time at Eden Prairie High School.

I am biased, but they turned out to be wonderful adults. All three are college graduates, one with a very successful business, another working in child and adult protection, and another employed in human resources for a large metro-area county.

Our two boys had different experiences in high school. They enjoyed their time as students at Eden Prairie despite the fact that their father was the assistant principal. They both have become successful professional men.

During the 1960s and Vietnam era, we had college students coming to the school and presenting the students with slips of papers explaining student rights. A few students took advantage and asked to see their records. Records were not secret. All students had to do was ask a counselor, and they would be happy to show the records, which were protected from anyone other than the student.

There was also an experience before we had an Eden Prairie police force. The school was protected by a constable, and in emergencies, the Minneapolis police were called. This particular afternoon, a gang of young men came to our school parking lot. I did see them and surmised from the way they looked and walked around with sticks that they were looking for trouble. I decided for the protection of our students that I had better go talk with them to see what they wanted. I went to the lot and confronted them as to why they were here. They were waiting for school to be dismissed. I told them we would not dismiss the students until they left the premises. They finally left and did not come back. I learned later they were part of a gang called the Kickers, with razor blades extended from the toes of their boots. Good thing they left peacefully.

A student was sent to the office by a teacher for disturbing her classroom. The teacher told me that the student kept tapping his pencil. When the teacher confronted him, he wouldn't stop, so he was sent to me. While I was talking to the student, I kept tapping my pencil on my desk. I asked what he did wrong to be sent to me, and his response was "Nothing." I kept tapping my pencil. He said the teacher was just having a bad day. I kept tapping and said that was unusual for this teacher because she was considered really good by most of the students. I kept tapping my pencil. Finally, the student said, "Will you stop tapping that pencil!"

I looked at him and said, "You got the message. Go to class tomorrow and be respectful to the teacher and yourself."

The boys started wearing their hair longer, and the girls' dresses kept getting shorter. At that time, parents who didn't like the dress and hairstyles suggested the school have a dress code. As assistant principal, I was assigned the job of monitoring this and sending girl violators home to change clothes. I called parents to let them know that Sue was coming home for a longer dress. They would say, "What is wrong with the one she is wearing?" I might say the dress was too short, and the mother would say, "She left wearing a long dress." The students caught on that if Mom and Dad didn't approve what they wore, they could put the minidress in a bag and put it in their locker. When the time was appropriate, they would change at school.

Boys' hair even had a length that was not acceptable. There were a couple of years when the boys' hair was studied to see that it was not below their ears. Girls' skirts were also measured for length. Those were signs of the time. In review, I thought it was a waste of time. This was that era when it was a reaction of society, not just Eden Prairie. Hairstyles, dress lengths, and appearances are so cyclical. In the sixty-one years I have been involved with youth, I have seen those characteristics change a minimum of three times.

During the twenty-first century, school officials watched boys' pants be worn so low they were barely hanging on, tattoos on girls and boys, and miniskirts come back. Now long hair is common among boys and men and technology has taken over the conversation.

I have tried to show that some youth test the system. Many don't, but I want to make a point that my experience shows they all like to succeed in something and to be recognized by someone who sincerely cares—someone who understands the individual's rights in dress or appearance, will take the time to listen, and is open-minded about their concerns. Times are always different, but I firmly believe the inner child is the same.

Chapter 7

. . . .

Student Achievement

To point out the achievements of students is difficult because, in my mind, most have been successful in their own way. Past students (1955–1986 graduates) that I met were living happy lives. Between the years 1955 and 1968, I knew the students as a teacher; from 1969 to 1986, they knew me as their assistant principal. From 1986 to the present, many have been good friends of mine, and we fish, golf, have coffee, and walk together.

I found a difference between the two (principal and teacher). A teacher's main purpose is to do his best to help the students learn a subject. The role of an administrator is to help students understand and reach the role they want in life. Establishing a comfortable learning environment is prime importance. An administrator is under scrutiny by parents, students, teachers, and other administrators. In analyzing decisions made, there is self-examination that may take place. Sometimes that self-evaluation is more difficult than what others may make.

An administrator does not get to know the students as closely as teachers do. Interactions with students are more sporadic, and unless there is a reason to spend more time with an administrator, students don't really get to know the principal.

The job provided me with several opportunities: arranging and practicing for graduation; attending most of the athletic, drama, and music activities; and supervising all dances, homecomings, proms, and Sadie Hawkins events during the year. I had my own homeroom group of students, which was enjoyable. I would bring donuts or sweet rolls of some kind until one of the young women said it might be better not to because of the sugar content that early in the school day before classes. Besides that, it was fattening. You always learn so much from youth. I also was involved with the student council and the National Honor Society at different times during my stint as an administrator.

A teacher's job is to motivate the students in class to learn the selected subject to the best of their ability. A teacher is with students basically every school day for the entire year and gets to know the students very well. A teacher learns their good and bad moods and determines whether something traumatic has happened so their minds are not on class. Their personal temperament, mental ability, motivation, and other feelings are not ignored. Teaching is never boring, even though the teacher has taught the same subject for many years. Students present a different challenge every day, but the teacher is responsible for everything that happens. The teacher is the leader in the classroom.

Two individuals who graduated from Eden Prairie felt so strongly about the school and community that they came back to give their expertise to help the school develop into even a better school then when they were there. Cindy Hayes and Conn McCarten were graduates that came back as principals at the high school. Cindy came first and then Conn followed her as principal. Recently, many alumni have returned as teachers and coaches in Eden Prairie schools.

Several students in my biology classes did follow through with their interest in biology and became high school or college teachers of biology. Others continued their study after college and became doctors and nurses.

A father of one of the students was on the school board at the time Mary and I were hired as teachers at Eden Prairie in 1955. I taught and coached his son, who later became Supreme Court Justice for the state of Minnesota. Paul Anderson retired after serving in that office many years. His sister, Mary, became a successful biology teacher.

Tom Anderson, a cousin of Paul and Mary, was in my first Industrial Arts class in 1955. He is one of the local residents who has lived in Eden Prairie all his life. Tom is very active with family, the Eden Prairie Lion Club, church, and the community.

The Boyd family of girls lived on a horse farm in Eden Prairie. They were all avid riders and taught others to ride as well. One of the family worked with horses and played the guitar in her adult life. Eden Prairie had other horse farms as well. In the late fifties and very early sixties, Eden Prairie had more horses per capita than any other community in Hennepin County.

A young man named Bob Remus was bigger in size than most players on our early football team. As coaches, we did everything to get him to be aggressive while playing football. Bob was afraid that because of his size, he would hurt someone. We told him the  other team's players had pads on like he did and not to worry; he should just go ahead and block or tackle as hard as he could. He still was a little reluctant until after graduation. He started professional wrestling under the tutelage of Verne Gagne, a well-known professional who did training in a barn on Pioneer Trail in Eden Prairie. Bob became a well-known wrestler throughout the country under a stage name of Sgt. Slaughter. In 2016 he is still active in arranging meets for the WWE (World Wrestling Entertainment, formerly WWF).

Sever Peterson was active in sports while in school, but he was also active in learning the farming business from a successful farming father. They would grow vegetables and deliver them for sale at the farmer's market in Minneapolis. After high school graduation, he went to the University of Minnesota to learn more about farming. Since then he has become well-known around the state for his Sever Sweet Corn Tents around shopping malls in the summer. They sell many other vegetables as well. He has gone to foreign countries, such as Korea and Brazil, to teach farming skills. These skills were not to change farming habits, but to teach the farmers how to take advantage of conditions for better production.

Ernie Shuldheis was an outstanding basketball player and trackman in the early sixties. He set a record for points scored in a basketball season, and for some time, he had the record for long jump and pole vault. He worked with Eden Prairie Historical Society and wrote a book on the history of Eden Prairie. He also wrote a column for the Historical Society about the history of what happened on a day during the week.

Leon Nesbitt was Eden Prairie's first football quarterback. After graduation, he went to Winona State University. Following graduation, he became successful in the insurance business. In his retirement, he has an apple orchard and catering business (and more) east of Prescott, Wisconsin.

Quarterback Kurt Woodhouse went to the Coast Guard Academy in New London, Connecticut. After graduation from the academy, he was the architect that designed the Twin Towers located at the corner of 494 and Highway 12 in Minnetonka, Minnesota.

An early trackman named Lynn was schooled in forestry and is active as a forester in the northwest states. His home was near what was called the Purple Barn just off 78th Street in eastern Eden Prairie. The barn had dance and wedding parties. It was quite nice. Eden Prairie High had the spring prom at the Purple Barn.

Our team doctor for many of the early years was Dr. Lineer. He had a son and daughter at Eden Prairie High. John was a very good football player. He also excelled in track, throwing shot put and discus. He held the record in the shot event for many years. He became doctor like his father and practiced in Houston, Texas. He was also involved in making his own chili to compete in the big Texas chili bake-off contests.

A young woman in my biology class was a member of an early Eden Prairie family. Her name was Barbara Bren, and her mother, Martha, was a secretary in the schools for many years. She was much loved by teachers and students. I remember Barbara because of her enthusiasm for everything and her drive to succeed. She had two brothers, Richard and Bruce, who had the same desire to do the best they could in everything they did.

Early on, two brothers, Jim and Glen Simons, had a strong interest in basketball. Every time I saw them, they had basketballs in their hands. They both were good high school players. You could always find them in the gym, shooting baskets.

A trackman had success after a near fatal episode. Chris had participated in football, basketball, and track. He was a sophomore running the hurdles at a meet in Waconia. He was a good hurdler, but the coach said he looked strange the way he ran the last two. At the end, he went to pick up his sweat clothes, but they would keep falling from his hand. The players noticed it and told the coach, who had him immediately sent to Waconia Hospital. Doctors from Mayo Clinic were there and identified the problem right away. He was sent by ambulance to the University of Minnesota Hospital.

Doctors diagnosed the location of a blood clot and thought the least amount of damage would occur if they operated. They removed a section of the skull so they could get at the clot. The clot was removed, and the piece of skull was put back in place. After a lengthy recovery, he was back in school. Due to the operation, he had some impairment with his right arm and right foot. After high school graduation, he attended St. Johns University. Following completion there, he attended Palmer School of Chiropractic. He graduated and is a very successful chiropractor in Connecticut. He was picked to represent the Connecticut chiropractors to the state legislature. His hobbies are competing in triathlons and bike racing. Dr. Gary Pennebaker was his mentor.

Jill graduated from Eden Prairie High and from the University of Minnesota. She entered a business helping people find jobs and helping businesses find employees. After working for a company for ten years, she decided to start a business of her own. She went to St. Thomas Business School and learned the financial and organizational techniques to operate her own business. She started her own business called NEXPRO and now has expanded her offices, one in St. Louis Park and another in Shakopee, Minnesota.

Sean loved doing artwork. Joey Terriquez, the art teacher in the high school, was an inspiration to continue his art skills. After high school, he attended Minneapolis School of Art and Design. In Savannah, Georgia, he completed his master of fine arts degree. His interest in art also includes science.

Sean has displayed art in many galleries throughout Minneapolis and neighboring cities. His work included building a seven-foot in diameter, four-thousand-pound floating biosphere sculpture, which was displayed in Lake Superior in Duluth Harbor. The model was built in response to a shortage of green space and actual climate change. He also is responsible for interaction between his neighborhood, the Minneapolis Park Board, City Council, and the governor of Minnesota to clean Lake Hiawatha of pollution that enters through storm sewers. He is a teacher of art at the University of Minnesota and also at St. Cloud University.

Ellen graduated from Eden Prairie and then earned a social work degree at Metro State. She then worked for Washington County in the Department of Child Protection. The job was very stressful, with many disturbing situations. She worked for ten years until marriage. Then her husband's job called for a transfer to Indian Wells, California. Ellen went to California and was employed by Riverside County in the district attorney's office for one year. For another thirteen years, Ellen worked in Adult Protection. She was challenged by many of the situations calling for police backup. Because of that, she enrolled in a public service academy and passed both the written and practical exams. Recently she joined the Fire Department of Idlewild, California.

Maureen graduated from Eden Prairie and then attended the University of Minnesota, graduating with a degree in Human Resources. She was the human resource representative for Banta Printing, Salzer Spine Tech, and, for the last thirteen years, Washington County, in Stillwater, Minnesota. She was involved in making several major decisions with police, fire, and other county workers.

The above five happen to be our children. We are proud of their success.

Many women and men from early Eden Prairie are serving in public life around the country. They are mayors of cities and a state senator.

L-R: Chris, Dad, Mother, Julia Sean, Maureen, Ellen

Eden Prairie city is fortunate to have several graduates working in various capacities. David Lindahl does great work as city economic development advisor. They are in as many diversified vocations as there are graduates. When I visited during class reunions, I learned that Eden Prairie graduates are prepared to move on in the world after high school. They appear to be happy, respectful, and talented.

Mary and I had a picnic at our home to honor the early football players, track competitors, and cheerleaders. We wanted to recognize their participation when Eden Prairie was a very small school and did not win trophies, but everyone practiced hard and played hard to do so. The teams played on makeshift fields early on and had no track, but they persevered.

Seventy people showed up at our home. I rented red-and-black tables and chairs, red-and-black utensils, and napkins, and set them up in the driveway. A caterer and helpers served food in the garage. People traveled from California, Utah, Colorado, Florida, Wisconsin, Iowa, and many parts of Minnesota. They had a wonderful time for a night and a day, seeing friends they had not seen in years.

The crowd was an example of successful graduates, but most of all, they were happy and friendly. Three former student-athletes were responsible for the gathering: Wayne Kopesky took charge of invitations and did the photo work of all early teams and cheerleaders, plus publishing the records for football; Tony Chevalier and his wife, Joanie, were responsible for displays; Lloyd Engler and his wife, Andrea, did overall planning and helped with everything that needed to be done. Much history was talked about over those two days.

There are so many more successes, and I have highlighted a few. Almost all alumni that I meet are happy, positive adults. Eden Prairie parents have always had high expectations for their children, whether it be professional, vocational, or avocational. I enjoy attending class reunions and hearing about individual's lives and families. One alumnus questioned me about how it felt to have all your past students on Medicare. I do remember a majority of the students over my teaching time period, and I appreciate their impact on my life.

Chapter 8

Tom's Story

Following twelve years of teaching biology, industrial arts, and physical education, as well as subjects for Adult Community Education in a small but growing community, I became an administrator. One of the many assignments was to maintain order. Another was to see that students improved their learning by attending classes. One young fellow (whom I will call Tom) was having a difficult time attending his assigned classes regularly. It was not due to any physical or mental abnormality, but a choice.

I spoke with him several times regarding his skipping. It became necessary, in my mind, that he be sent home for a couple of days to let his mother inform him why he was in school.

Following the short suspension, I called him into my office. I explained to him that if he was going to be in the building, it was his responsibility to attend classes on a regular basis. I called Tom's mother and asked that she come to school with him if he skipped again. She said that she would be more than happy to do so.

I relayed the information to Tom by saying, "If you miss another class, which is your choice, I will send you home. Your mother will bring you back the next day and be with you until she thinks you can get to your class alone."

Tom missed his next class, so I called him to the office, telephoned his mother, and sent him home. Tom called me several times that evening, saying, "I will not come to school with my mom."

My response was, "Sorry, Tom, but you made the choice."

The next morning, no Tom. I called his mother, who said that he wouldn't come to school if she were coming along. I said, "We can't let him get by with that. Would you mind if I come over?"

She said, "Come on over. He's still in bed."

When I arrived, sure enough, he was still in bed. With his mother's permission, I knocked on the bedroom door and told Tom that I was coming in. I sat by his bed and said, "Tom, you have to come to school."

He answered, "Not with my mom."

I said, "You made the choice."

Since he was refusing to come, I went to the phone to dial the police. "Please come to this address and bring a truant student to school."

Hearing this, he said, "All right, then I will go." I left the bedroom while he got dressed for school. Mother, Tom, and I drove to school.

I had previously notified Tom's teachers to have an extra chair for his mother and to welcome her. At noon, I called both to the office and thanked his mother for coming and Tom for going to all his classes. I excused the mother for the rest of the day. I told Tom I was happy for him and realized that he didn't want me to talk about this in front of his buddies. I said, "When you attend all your classes regularly, and I see you in the hall, I will casually brush against you and you will know that I know."

Tom never missed another class the rest of the year. Following graduation from high school, he attended the University of Minnesota, Duluth. At the beginning of his senior year, he was elected class president. Tom then went on to graduate from law school, opening an office in St. Paul. I sent flowers to his office on opening day, with a note congratulating him on his success.

We have visited often since that time after high school. We are friends and meet to have coffee.

Chapter 9

The Administrator's Role

I became part-time assistant principal in 1968 while still teaching a smaller load of biology. I was making the transition from teaching tenth-grade students biology in the classroom to teaching all students in the building. The subject was to respect others and yourself, have compassion and understanding of classmates, be positive, listen to teachers, not harm others physically or verbally, and motivate yourself. And of course, we discussed studying hard and keeping your grades as high as your capabilities will allow for more success in the future.

I was the assistant principal from 1968 through 1986. I worked with four principals, including Norm Nelson and Paul Schee. Following them was David Flannery, a principal from a North Minneapolis school, followed by Arne Johnson, a principal in the Robinsdale school district. The school board evidently thought it best to bring in an outsider with ideas from other districts. We were a dynamic, growing district during that time. I had the opportunity to familiarize the newcomers to our student body, community, teachers, curriculum, facilities, and working staff members, meaning clerical, cooks, and custodial.

Being a so-called old timer and performing a new responsibility as an administrator in the school, I was surprised at some of the crazy things with which I had to deal. Many wonderful things happened as well, of course.

When Bill broke a school rule and the penalty was suspension, that was my first experience in disciplining a student under the new principal's guidance. He spoke with the student and informed him that he would be suspended and sent home. The principal told him to leave the building and go home. I overheard the conversation and immediately spoke with the principal. I asked if he had called the parents to notify them. He had not. Then I asked how the student was supposed to get home. The principal said he could walk. I then stated the school was not in the city, but in the country. This area was thirty-six square miles, and the walk could be very long in the winter. He then called the parents and asked them to pick up Bill.

Another example of city experience versus Eden Prairie style was when the school was having a lyceum program in the gymnasium. In the past, the students would pay a quarter to the homeroom teacher to see the program. The teacher would then select a student to take the collected quarters to the office. When the new principal heard how the money was getting to the office, he said, "They can't do that because people could come into the building and rob them."

I responded by saying, "Not in Eden Prairie."

As a parent, I was somewhat at fault. If our children were being ridiculed on the bus by other students, they asked to ride to school with me. We wanted our children to be able to deal with unpleasant situations and resolve them themselves. I would break down sometimes and say okay. It must be realized that early on in the 1950s and early 1960s, our salaries were not at the top of the list. The cars I drove were functional but pretty ugly. With a growing family, that is not where we wanted to put our money. The car was an early 1940-model Plymouth purchased from my Grandfather Calhoun, and it was green. Some of the school kids called it the "green vomit," and it was recognized as our means of transportation.

So when the children came to school with me, not only were they embarrassed by the car, but also that they were with me. It was a teenage thing.

I was driving behind the bus, and a young fellow saw the car and proceeded to show his middle finger to me. I followed the bus to school, close enough that I could keep track of the rascal. As soon as the bus stopped at school, I immediately went into the bus and confronted the person. I explained that if he ever did that again when I had my family in the car, he would have to deal with me big time. My children were all hiding on the floor of my car, embarrassed. I understood, and they had my sympathy.

We had an experience with eggs thrown at our house. I belonged to a bowling league, and it was the Wednesday prior to Thanksgiving Day. Mary was home and heard something bump on the side of the house. As she walked out, she saw four boys going over the hill behind our house. She proceeded to go to the neighbors' houses and tell them their sons just threw eggs at our house. They didn't believe their sons would do anything like that until they saw them coming down from the hill. These were all boys in the high school and our neighbors. We were entertaining for Thanksgiving. The next morning, all four boys were at our house with pails of water, ladders, and scrub brushes that they brought from home. Immediately behind them were their fathers. They worked all morning. By the time our company arrived, the house was cleaner than ever. All materials, including the boys and their fathers, were gone.

Our oldest daughter was just starting first grade in the two-story main building of the school. She was the survivor of identical twins born seven weeks premature and had only weighed a little more than three pounds at birth. She had to stay in the hospital in an isolette for thirty days until they felt she was strong enough to come home. As a first grader, she was small in stature. She would ride the bus and would try to stay up with the rest of the children getting off the bus so she could enter the door with the others because she couldn't open the school doors by herself. One day, she couldn't keep up and got to the door alone. The secretary, who was the best and most caring woman, saw her and came to her rescue and helped her through the door. It was a memory that stuck with our daughter for sixty years. Mrs. Bren was loved by everyone. She sewed a button on Ellen's sweater, who then gave her the name "the sewing nurse."

Chapter 10

Discipline with Understanding

Assistant principal was my new role after teaching industrial arts, biology, and physical education, and coaching for twelve years. A part of the assignment was dealing with students who had difficulty in following school guidelines, teacher guidelines, or parent expectations.

My first experience in calling a parent regarding an infraction was a little scary. Mike was having some narrow escapes from various teachers, but at this particular time, he left school and was walking down the road. The next hour, a teacher notified me that Mike was not in class. My duty then was to call the parent and let them know that Mike was skipping school.

As we were talking and I was explaining, I heard the phone at the other end fall to the floor. Following that, I heard what sounded like a body collapsing to the floor and no answer on the phone.

I quickly told the principal what happened and stated I best go over and see if the mother was all right. When I arrived at her home, the father met me at the door, and I asked what happened. He explained that she had a problem with stress and that she would faint. The call evidently pushed her over the edge. Fortunately, she was not injured in the fall and they were able to convince the son to stay in school. Good work, parents.

Another incident that comes to mind regards a parent knowing his child and believing what he says. I was on duty to supervise the lunchroom! After lunch, as students were leaving for class, I noticed a young man throwing a carton of milk against the wall over the exit door. The smashed carton sent milk spattering down on the students unlucky enough to be using that exit door. I clearly saw the whole episode and called the student into my office. I phoned the father to let him know that his son would be suspended for a couple of days to think it over.

That evening, I received a call from the dad, saying, "My son said he didn't do it and he has never lied to me before. I am sure he is not lying now."

I stated that this might be the first time. "Please bring him back to school the day after tomorrow."

When he did come back, we discussed the problem of not accepting responsibility for what he did and the mess it caused. He said he was sorry. The father understood that it was not healthy for the individual to get out of something by not taking responsibility for his actions. Mike was forgiven and served his time. He was welcomed back to school. This was a good lesson for all.

Hanging on the wall behind my desk was a picture of a Raggedy Ann doll with a smiling face. Under the picture was a short saying: "The truth will set you free." Many times, if a student was sent to the office by a teacher, he would be defensive (a natural state) and say, "I didn't do anything." I think I have heard just about every kind of student excuse.

If I knew for sure the student did something and was just making alibis, I often would point to the picture and watch the reaction. Most of the time, after looking at the picture and the saying, they would say something like, "I don't know what I was thinking," or "I am sorry. I will not do that again." If that didn't work, I would ask if it was necessary to call a parent. Some might not care. Others would plead, "Please don't." I understood in a very few cases why they did not want me to make the call. Some parents could not handle a child breaking a rule, whether it be disrespect to a teacher, bullying a student, or any other regulation. A small minority of parents would get physical or use verbal abuse. In those cases, the punishment was kept in school.

One of the roles of an administrator is to teach what is and what is not acceptable in school. We understand that these are growing children and will make mistakes. I call it "discipline with understanding." Because someone makes a mistake once does not mean he is a bad person. Our duty is to help him understand that.

The majority of parents are thoughtful and supportive of the school. They support the school by attending functions and by supporting teachers and their decisions. Parents are supportive by also passing school bond referendums. Here in Eden Prairie, that has been unprecedented. That support has helped to build ten schools and to keep the schools at the upper level of performance in the state.

Chapter 11

Winter Activities as a Teacher

Snow days were quite frequent in the early days of the 1950s. Many times, after a big snowstorm, school officials had to wait for the county to do the plowing and open the roads before we could say school was on. Still a township, Eden Prairie did not have the luxury of big snowplows.

On one occasion when school was called off early in the day, children were sent home before a big storm hit the area. So often, especially in outstate schools where most students are bussed in, the decision is based on the weather forecast. A decision is usually made by the superintendent of schools, in cooperation with the police and the weatherman. That decision is a tough one, but once made, there is no turning back. Sometimes the predicted bad storm turns out to be a beautiful, sunshiny day.

Such was the case one day in Eden Prairie when the children were sent home early one morning. Teachers worked in their rooms, correcting papers, doing lesson plans, or cleaning. Lunchtime came, so many of us decided to go to Chanhassen for lunch. We knew that we would not be in touch with students the rest of the day. A young group of teachers in their twenties from neighboring schools was also there. After lunch, we were given a challenge to a snowball fight. We could not turn that down, so here were all these teachers from four or five neighboring schools, in the middle of the street, having a snowball fight.

One might say that this was not very professional or that we were doing this on school time. In our minds, we had done our job for the district before we came to lunch. Anyway, we were having a good time on a snow vacation day, just enjoying ourselves.

One of the board members was not at home because of the storm threat. He was in Chanhassen. He saw what we were doing in the snowball fight and immediately drove to school to report our activity to the principal. Our principal, Mr. Martinka, was a well-loved administrator who respected his teachers. He listened to the board member's description of what we teachers were doing. Then he replied, "Yes, aren't they a great group?" What more to say.

Sometimes being an administrator, teacher, minister, or anyone in a position of authority can put the child and parent in uncomfortable situations. A personal one was during the 1960s, when beer parties were popular with kids. Eden Prairie was still undeveloped, with a low population count, creating many open fields.

Some children would locate an open field that could be reached by automobile through the field roads. Someone with a van would load a keg of beer, and away they would go with cars following them to this hidden field.

Their movements did not go unnoticed by the new Eden Prairie Public Safety Department. Officials knew where these hidden places were. Some officers might have been searching for areas themselves when they were in high school, before joining the Public Safety Department.

On this particular night, two of our daughters were with a group of friends at one of these parties. As parents, we had no idea of any of this. About eleven o'clock that night, I got a call from Public Safety asking if I would come to the police station to pick up two daughters and two of their girlfriends whose parents were not at home. Upset and angry as I was, I went to the police station to pick them up. The girls were behind bars, along with many others. The officer excused them to me. I walked to my car with four teenagers, two on each side, hand in hand. The story was that the police came, and those who saw them early and were fast enough took off running and got away. Several did not, and I had four of them.

The next morning, Police Chief Jack Hacking came to school, which he often did, and said to me, "I saw you last evening, Curt, but you didn't look like you were in the mood to talk." How true!

Experiences are a part of life. Mary and I have five children. All have had their moments, but you can't find one of them who isn't a loving, caring, understanding, and successful adult with successful children of their own. One is not married and teaches at the University of Minnesota and also at St. Cloud University.

Our home was toward the end of a dead-end gravel road, which had a big, open field at the end. Every so often in the evening, a van would come down the road, followed by a group of cars full of young people. Inside the van would be a keg of beer. Soon the police would visit, and the van would go back out the dusty road, followed by the cars and the police. Another beer party broken up.

One winter evening, Mary and I were hosting a faculty get-together. Around eleven, a young man knocked on our door. He said, "Mr. Connaughty, could I use your phone to call a tow truck because my car is stuck in a snow bank at the end of the road."

I said, "I have a couple of snow shovels. Let us see if we can shovel your car out."

As we were walking in the dark with shovels over our backs, he said, "I have to tell you that I have a girl in the car."

My response to him was, "I sure hope so. I would hope you wouldn't be on this dead-end road in the middle of the winter by yourself." He was relieved. We dug the car out easily, and they went on their merry way.

Chapter 12

The End Is Not in Sight

I was in my thirty-first year of teaching, coaching, and administration at Eden Prairie High School and enjoying all the different experiences. Then I was notified by the TRA (Teachers Retirement Association) that they were extending an early retirement option called the "rule of 85." This meant that a teacher with thirty years of experience who was fifty-five years old could retire. It was thought by teachers like me, who fell into that category, that districts wanted to retire those at the higher end of the pay scale to make room for beginning teachers at the lower end. Whether that was the real reason or not, teachers who loved their work felt that way. The plan was so good that it was very hard to refuse. Some were very happy with it, but I knew many who were sorry to leave education. Realistically, it was difficult not to accept the financial retirement. I was one who thought that I gave up something I truly loved for money.

On the other hand, I remember certain meetings with parents when someone would ask a question and the response of another teacher might be, "Refer that to Mr. Connaughty. He has been here forever." I was a senior member with years of experience in the district at the time. I was not the oldest in age, but I had a number of years in Eden Prairie. I started believing that I was getting old, and that was encouragement enough to accept the retirement. As I look back, of course, fifty-five is just a youngster in the prime of life.

I have in my life taught biology, industrial arts, and physical education. Each subject was an enjoyment, and I felt they were self-motivating subjects for students.

Adults wanted to learn also, so I taught various courses of their interest in evening classes. One was after the atomic bomb was dropped, and people were very nervous that it could happen here. I taught adult classes on protecting yourself against radiation, and how to build and stock a fallout shelter. Three shelters were built by class members on their property.

During my years in physical education, many units of different activities were taught to at least familiarize students with the fundamentals. The major sports of basketball and football were included, but we also had volleyball, soccer, wrestling, gymnastics, track, camping, golf, badminton, and dancing. Dancing was taught in conjunction with girls' physical education, taught by Dorothy McIntyre.

Miss McIntyre was the leader for girls' equal opportunity in athletics. The history of her work is represented today by an equal number of sports. I remember the difficulty she had in convincing male coaches in the state that it was time to allow girls to practice and play in their gyms. It was not easy to convince them that girls needed gym time and space equal to boys. She later took a job with the Minnesota State High School League, where she fulfilled her drive for equal participation for girls in the state of Minnesota.

I coached as an assistant in basketball. I started football in 1957 and track in 1958. I also coached baseball for one year.

First Row: D. Moe, L. Woodward, D. Nesbitt, K. Kearney
Second Row: D. Pomerleau, H. Duda, B. Roaderick, T. Roeser, D. Schmidt, G. Stodola, D. Hirt
Third Row: J. Balfanz, B. Pauly, B. Roaderick, J. Roeser, D. Ravnholdt, L. Nesbitt, Mr. Connaughty
Fourth Row: D. Kormylo, D. Larson, M. Susemihl, S. Roe, R. Wrigley

I became full-time assistant principal in 1969. Our early athletic conference was the Minnesota Valley Conference. During the early 1970s, Eden Prairie joined the Suburban West, and in the late 1980s, we moved to the Lake Conference. Around 2013, members of the Lake Conference decided to start a new conference, which they did, but left Eden Prairie out of their conference. Therefore, Eden Prairie joined the Classic Lake, with four other West Metro schools: Edina, Hopkins, Minnetonka, and Wayzata. They now belong to the West Metro conference.

Eden Prairie had grown from 13 graduates in the 1956 graduating class to 920 seniors at their peak. The school was the largest in the state. During the 2005–2006 school year, the total school population was 9,897.

Eden Prairie has won the Football Lake Conference title eighteen of twenty years, and many more football championships and conference and state titles since Mike Grant has become the football coach and activity director; and our student body has become one of the largest in the state. Other schools are close but have not had the consistent football success Eden Prairie has had in the last twenty years.

My career of daily activity in school ended in 1986, but I am still involved with Eden Prairie schools by operating the clock during football season and starting track meets there and around the metro area. The year 2016 will mark my sixty-first year of service to the Eden Prairie schools.

You might ask why I stayed in one school system my whole life. The answer is that every year was almost like being in a new school. New students were coming every year, schools were being built, the curriculum was changing, sports were improving, staff kept growing, and administration kept changing. To me, it was an ideal situation, and I have truly enjoyed my life here.

Before retiring, I was thinking of another career to keep me busy. Since one of my majors was industrial arts, I thought that experience might be complimentary to the real estate business.

A couple of former students were in the real estate business.

One was Richard Bergman, an agent for Merrill Lynch's real estate division. He was a big reason why I chose real estate. I had already completed my state licensing to become an agent.

The day I left school, I was employed by Merrill Lynch real estate in Edina. That first day was my first sale of a townhome to the principal of North Junior High in Hopkins.

Ralph Burnet took over Merrill Lynch after Merrill Lynch dropped their real estate division. Burnet Realty was the company for several years. Coldwell Banker bought out Burnet, so the company was called Coldwell Banker Burnet. I then moved to their Eden Prairie office, where I retired after fifteen years in the real estate business.

I enjoyed real estate, but it was different from my life in education. One big difference was during lunch period in school, I was surrounded by people: teachers, students, and staff. Soon, after I had a few days of adjustment in real estate, I was by myself, previewing homes. I stopped for lunch at a Dairy Queen and ordered a milk shake and a chili dog. I went to a park to eat. Looking around, I saw that I was all alone. I thought, *what was I thinking, leaving a great job and seeing all those people in the school lunchroom?* Mine was a lonely lunch that day.

Our family now consists of five children: Ellen, Julia, Maureen, Christopher, and Sean. There are ten grandchildren: Aaron, Emily, Max, Rose, Patty, Sarah, Austin, Dan, Spencer and Abbie. Six great-grandchildren: Macie, Parker, Cora, Mae, Sylvie, and Jack.

I enjoy many other activities. Golfing, exercise with a walking group, Lifetime Health Club workouts, Lion's Club, and a fishing group called the Mixed Nuts. The name came from a group of fathers taking their sons fishing, thus called Mixed Nuts. The fathers have since died, but the group continues, with new people joining for the houseboat fishing experience in Canada every spring. During the summer, traveling, gardening and golf are fun activities for me.

I am involved with school activities and sports at all levels. I enjoyed my years in education. I learned a lot from students over the years and hope they learned from me as a teacher, coach, and administrator. Some students and I might have had unpleasant experiences, but hopefully, we learned from those times. I have no resentments toward anyone, and I hope the same is true of them. I love them all and am happy when I get to see them now as parents and grandparents. Memories from the past about school will never be forgotten.

> My learning has been both professional and personal, marked by my increasing belief in understanding of diversity and openness of communication. To parents, grandparents, and friends in the adult world, I say learn from these young people.
>
> —CSC

I enjoy my new life, and I'll stay busy because the end is not in sight! I have things to accomplish with family, friends, community, and schools.

Kindness to others will bring kindness to you.

—CSC

Memories

High School campus

Old School Administration

CLASSES

First Row: P. Eames, P. Kocourek, A. Gilbert, M. Marshall, E. Florez, R. Christenson, P. Fisher

Second Row: Mr. Connaughty, B. Kormylo, R. Hirt, B. Moe, J. Pomerleau, P. Boyd, B. Kopesky, M. Wenisch

Third Row: B. Filpi, J. Simons, K. Foss, B. Listberger, T. Smith, W. Chevalier, L. Parrish, B. Pierce

First Row: Mr. Connaughty, D. Florez, M. Nelson, J. Holasek, G. Holasek, D. Shilda, K. Varpness, F. Schutrop, K. Lubrant

Second Row: A. Penny, K. Brown, S. Fillipi, W. Good, B. Kopesky, G. Holasek, M. Boyd, J. Palveka, B. Bren

Third Row: B. Foss, C. Monson, J. Balfanz, B. Brekke, M. Susemihl, D. Jacques, H. Duda, J. Fisher, J. Lueck

ACTIVITIES

First Row: B. Row, L. Brekke, L. Phillips, J. Moran, A. Ravnholdt, M. Kaye

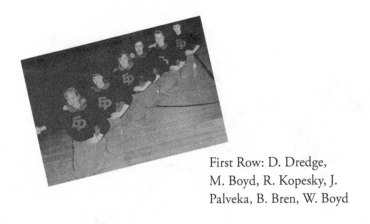

First Row: D. Dredge, M. Boyd, R. Kopesky, J. Palveka, B. Bren, W. Boyd

1959 Pep Club

1960 Glee club

1960 Glee Club

1960 Sadie Hawkins

1961 Junior Class Play

1963 Seniors

1960 Faculty Fred, Susan, Curt

 1960 Faculty Mrs. Stewart

Kids Cheering

1957 B Team Basketball

1958 B Team Basketball

1959 B Team Basketball

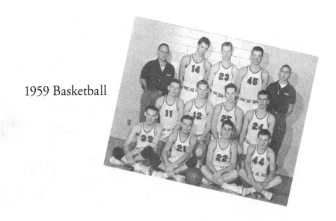

1959 Basketball

1959 Football Team

1959 Baseball Team

1959 Track Team

1960 Track Team

1961 Basketball Team

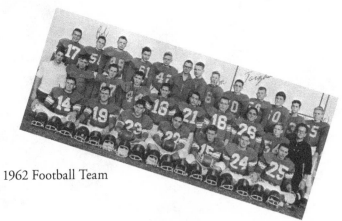

1962 Football Team

1963 Track Team

1964 Track Team

1965 Track Team

1965 Basketball Team

1965 Football Team

1966 Football Team

1963 Band

1961 Football Team

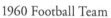

1968 Football Team

1960 Football Team

1963 Football Team

1964 Football Team

Bits of the Consolidated School History

The school first opened in March 1924.

The first school paper was published in October 1926 and called the *Buzzer*; the name was changed to the *Eyrie* in September of 1961.

The first homecoming was February 13, 1931. Eden Prairie beat Bloomington 29–16.

Homecoming was held during the basketball season; in 1958 it was switched to football.

Until 1958, baseball and basketball were the only Eden Prairie sports. In 1958 football and track were added and in 1962 wrestling.

The first football team had fourteen players.

In March 1927, the Eden Prairie girls' basketball team beat Bloomington 48–0.

At the athletic banquet in May 1931 the first EP letters were given out.

In June 1939 a tornado hit the school.

The first homecoming queen, Dorothy Klinglehutz, was crowned in February 1940.

The gym was used as a community movie theater in the late '20s and early '30s.

The bleachers supposedly could hold four hundred people.

The scarlet and black school colors were adopted in 1928.

Some prominent teachers and when they started teaching—Dotty Nye (1933), Conley Engstrom (1937), Martha Wanek (1943), Curt Connaughty (1955), Dorothy McIntyre (1959), Emmett Stark (1960), and John Ryski (1963).

From 1929 to 1966 Eden Prairie graduated 838 students. In 1961 total enrollment K–12 was 840. In 2004, 847 students graduated.

Prior to 1937, Eden Prairie didn't have a mascot. Sanford Dean (EPHS '39) recalls, "We grew tired of being referred to as the Eden Prairie lads or the lads from Eden Prairie. One day while sitting in chem lab we decided we needed a name. We noticed that a lot of sport teams had the name, the Eagles. Eden Prairie Eagles sounded good and no one around here used the name, we figured it would be a good fit."

In 1951, the north addition, affectionately known as the "Sheep Shed," was completed.

In 1957, the west addition was added.

The 1960 class was the last class to graduate from the stage of the old consolidated school.

The first graduation was an eighth grade graduation held in June 1924.

The student council of 1931 felt the need for a new basketball song. They offered prizes for the best song, and Lucy Kortz won the contest.

The Original 1931 Version	2004 Version
And when the Scarlet men go dribbling by, The cheering hundreds should their battle cry, For Eden Prairie is marching on the floor, Fighting the game for you ever more. And when the offense men go sneaking through, They'll sweep the defense man aside, When Eden Prairie fights for victory, Then Eden Prairie will win the game. V-I-C-T-O-R-Y, VICTORY, VICTORY YEA! EAGLES!	And when the Eagle teams come marching by, The cheering hundreds should their battle cry, For Eden Prairie Eagles are the team, That's fighting the fight for you RAH! RAH! And when the red and black are on our side, The Eagles spirit never dies, For Eden Prairie fights for victory, And to win this game. V-I-C-T-O-R-Y, VICTORY, VICTORY YEA! EAGLES!

The cheer/song was set to the tune of the "Washington and Lee Swing."

During the basketball games prior to 1940, the score was kept on a blackboard on the stage. In 1940 they got a scoreboard.

The first yearbook/annual was put out in 1944.

Companies first started putting paint in aerosol cans in the mid-1950s; this is also about the same time students started painting "Graffiti Bridge."

The student council was organized in 1931.

Sno-Daze was first held in February 1961.

In November 1961 the Lettermen's Club was organized.

During the early years, the basketball team didn't have a school bus to take them to the away games; the coach used his car to transport them. In February 1929, Mr. Sherman Mitchell, while taking the players home, got his car stuck at the Riley Lake M & St. L. crossing, and a freight train totaled out his car. No one was hurt.

July 2004
Ernie Shuldhiess (EPHS '66)
Eden Prairie Historical Society

CPSIA information can be obtained
at www.ICGtesting.com
Printed in the USA
LVHW092149180520
656008LV00006B/81/J